BREXIT'S A TRICK
NOT A TREAT?

MIKE CASHMAN

If you hoped for a Brexit that's sweet
As a cake you can have and can eat,
Do you now realise
The extent of the lies,
And that Brexit's a trick, not a treat?

Mike Cashman

FOREWORD

The absurdities and contradictions of our politics first motivated me, in 2016, to highlight them in song.

Perhaps we all need to lighten up a little. There are serious matters to deal with, but can we also see the funny side?

If we can look at real events with some amusement as well as fervent support or opposition, then perhaps, in our dialogue, we may see some more smiles and fewer frowns.

Public lies can be funny. They can also be tragic and damaging, but still funny based on the "You have to laugh or you'd cry" principle. There are those who feel that "Remain lied too", and so there is a song just for them. But this book is my personal reaction to events, and at times my own guesswork as to our leaders' thoughts. Don't take it too seriously.

Is our situation serious? Yes. The five lines of "Brexit's a Trick, not a Treat" sum this up, and make this the title song. Like other pieces, it is intended to inform as well as amuse.

I hope you enjoy what follows. And for those who have expressed their appreciation when some of these individual items have been shared, thank you.

Mike Cashman
September 2019

LAYOUT

The dates shown are the dates on which the pieces were written – sometimes a few days after the news story.

Where I have adapted a well-known song, I have included the name of the original song, though I expect most are obvious. It is pleasing how often an original fits so well, and "Maggie May" is my favourite in this respect. My thanks go to the original, talented writers and performers.

The original lyrics (for each song I have imitated) and recordings of it should be available online in most cases. For most songs the words here should match the tune exactly, so you should be able to karaoke them if you would like to. Occasionally I have included an extra verse or two compared to the original.

But you may also notice that not everything is a song or a poem, and not all the pieces are about Brexit. That's bonus material.

And this collection includes a brilliant guest contribution, "I am the Very Model of a Prejudiced Etonian", from the talented Robin Wallington.

We hope you enjoy reading and singing these pieces.

CONTENTS

1. The Referendum **5**
   Brexitian Fantasy 5
   Our Way 8
   Brexit Alphabet 10
   Cricket Scoreboard 12

2. Article 50 .... **13**
   Brexit Cokey 13
   Remain Lied Too 16
   You're in EU, Going for Exit 20
   Now She Is A Leaver 22
   Knowing Me Knowing EU 24
   EU Responds to Article 50. 26

3. Apologies Due (Election/Trump) **28**
   Maggie May 28
   I Beg My Pardon 31

4. Brexit Reflections **33**
   Brexit Pie 33
   When the Nightmare Is Over 38
   Say Goodbye Our Former Partner 41
   Where Have All of UKIP Gone? 43
   Could We Start Again Please? 44

5. More Brexit Realities **45**
   Don't Cry for Leave Now, Theresa 45
   Brexit Mia 47
   The Brexit Game 49
   Round - Like a Brexit Without Exit 51

6. **World Cup Fever** 53
   This Time 53
   Brexit's Coming Home (Three Lines on the Whip) 55
   Once More onto the Pitch, Dear Friends, Once More 57

7. **Heck it's Chequers – and Trump** 59
   19th Brexit Breakdown 59
   Trumpet So Wide 61
   It's My Brexit and I'll Cry if I Want to 63
   I'm Just A Girl Who Cain't Say "Go" 64
   How Do You Solve A Problem Like Our Brexit? 66
   Whatever Happened to The Brexit Deal? 68

8. **Preparing to Leave** 70
   Port-A-Loo 70

9. **Results of the Cluster-Interaction** 72
   Brexit's a Trick, not a Treat? 72
   Doh, We're Here 72
   Rock Paper Scissors 73

10. **Theresa May Battles On** 74
    Oh, Theresa First Looked Out 74
    The First No Deal 78
    Dance for the Deal 80
    They Said There'll Be Deals at Brexit. 82
    You're Got Brexit, Needing an Exit 83
    Take a Chance on Me. 84

11. **The last days of Theresa May** 87
    The Many Votes of Brexit 87
    Menu for EU Summit Dinner 89

Sit on the Fence 91
Final Say 91
I Might as Well Reign until September. 92
Parachute Drop 93

12. The Tory Party Leadership Context **94**
Seven Chaps Crave Loner Idiot Test 94
Channel 4 No-Show 94
Shove out his Ex? 94

13. European Parliament **95**
Ode to Misery 95

14. Boris takes charge **97**
Oh, I'll GATT By with a Little Help from My
Friends. 97
The Emperor with No Clothes 99
Under the Bus 99
Mars Bars and Crisps 100
ERG 100
The Bus with Smiling Faces 101
Send in the Boris Clowns 102
Britons Never, Never, Never Shall be Fooled. 104

15. No Deal again **105**
Onward Brexit No-Dealers 105
Try A Yellow Hammer 108
Denmark 110
Remainers Unite! 110
Thirty Days 110
'Till Borisma Drives The Backstop Far Away 111
Though I've Listened Long Enough to You 113

16. Cummings, Rees-Mogg and Proroguing **114**
    The Consensus of Cummings 114
    We're Off to See the Cummings 115
    As Long Jacob Slumbered 116
    Twenty-One Could Not Have Been Wronger 116
    Early Election 116
    Rees-Mogg Takes You Down 117
    I am the Very Model of a Prejudiced Etonian 119
    Government's Leader Says Government's Busy 121

17. Last Word (for now) **123**
    I Dreamed a Dream 123

Reference **125**
Index of titles 125
Index of references to original songs 128

1. The Referendum
Brexitian Fantasy

13 June 2016

I was prompted to write this shortly before the EU referendum, honestly quite staggered that the Leave side initially engaged in the economic debate, and, as far as I can see saw that they were losing the debate and switched arguments to "Nothing matters except sovereignty", which is where the song concludes.

The song also predicts the damage to sterling, and the reality that we will not be able to trade as well outside the EU, i.e. that trade deals would not be easy.

Is this the real thing?
Is this just fantasy?
Caught in a Farage
Escaped from reality,
Open your eyes
Look out for the lies and see.
I'm just a voter, I need no clarity,
Because I'm EC done, EC go,
Boris high, sterling low,
Any way the pound goes, doesn't really matter to me, to me.

Brexit, just stuffed the pound,
Got the rumour posted live,
Let the currency just dive.
Brexit, we were getting there

But then we went and threw it all away.
Britain, ooh-ooh-ooh
Didn't mean to make you cry.
If we're not afloat again this time tomorrow
Carry on, carry on, as if nothing really matters.

Too late, we blew it all.
Sent shivers down my spine.
There's Boris on the line.
Goodbye, economy, now got to go
Gotta leave you all behind and face the truth.
Britain, ooh-ooh-ooh
Did we want to go?
I sometimes wish no referendum at all.

I see a little fantasy of a plan
Boris J, Boris J, did you have a plandango?
Fantasy financial
Very insubstantial
Nigel Farage, Nigel Farage
In procession to Brecession
Nigel Farage did the damage
Catastrophage

Now we're a poor state, not much we're earning,
They're just a poor state, took the wrong turning.
Spare them and let them back into this EC
Oh, we voted out back then, will you let us in
Again? No, we will not let you in. Let us in!
Oh please? No, we will not let you in. Let us in!
Just once? No, we will not let you in. Let us in

Will not let you in. (Let us in!)
Never, never let you in
Never let you back in, oh.
No, no, no, no, no, no, no.
Oh, mama mia, mama mia (Mama mia, let me in.)
Boris Farage has no plan put aside for me, for me, for me.

So you think you can leave us and have the same trade?
So you think it's like you're in if you haven't paid?
Oh, Britain, should have thought of this June 2016,
When all that you said was "just gotta get right outta here".
(Oh, ooh, oh ooh)
Nothing really matters,
Except sovereignty,
Nothing really matters,
Nothing really matters to me.
Any way the wind blows.

Inspired by: *Bohemian Rhapsody*

Despite 400 shares the song above didn't sway the vote towards Remain, and in the immediate aftermath some voiced their regrets.

Our Way

25 June 2016

And so, the vote was done,
We listened to Farage concession.
He said, Remain had won,
He'd missed his chance, to lead Brecession.
They counted every vote.
To beat Remain would seem a far way;
But more, much more than this, we'd do it Our Way.

Bregrets, we've had a few -
They are so sad – we have to mention.
We thought we weren't lied to, that all was true, without exception.
We hoped - for hospitals - just one a week - and just down our way.
And so, to spend that cash, we voted Our Way.

Yes, there were times, I'm sure you knew,
When we bit off more than we could chew;
Oh, heck we won, what is that sound?
Stock market fell. What crashed the pound?
But through it all, when there was doubt,
We thought PM would sort it out -
Who, Gove-implored, fell on his sword, so now where's our way?

We followed Gove and all the chorus,
The JCB bloke, and crazy Boris.

And now, as tears are flowing,
And friends ask, "You really going?"
That protest vote, that "more or less now",
Has left us in this dreadful mess now;
Oh no, oh no not us, so was this Our Way?

For what is England, what have we got?
Some countries with us, or maybe not?
And so you vote, just how you feel - tomorrow is another deal.
We placed our votes.
We gave our quotes;
We voted Our Way

Inspired by: *My Way*

For the related news story look at Independent article "Anger over 'Bregret' as Leave voters say they thought UK would stay in EU".

Brexit Alphabet

21 October 2016

*It turned out that Boris didn't have any sort of plandango,
which gave rise to the events described below.*

A is for Article - 50 - big fuss.
B is for Brexit and Boris and Bus.
C is for Cameron and Credit rating (gone).
D - David Davis, the new Brexit Don.
There's E in EU and at present we're in it.
There's F in Farage who'll be gone in a minute.
And G is for Gove, who thinks experts a pity;
H is for Hilary, chairs the committee.
I is for Ireland, concerned for the border.
J is for Juncker, who runs EU order.
K is for Kingdom, united for now;
L is for Liam, who'll fix trade somehow.
M is for May, with no commentary running,
N for Negotiate, poker-faced, cunning.
O for Obama, his words some found hurting.
P is for Parliament, role is uncertain.
Q is for Question, that showed how we're broken.
And R Referendum - the people have spoken.
S is for Scotland and Sturgeon and Stuck.
T is for Treaty - we'll fix this with luck.
U is for Union - like it or not?
V is the Vote to reject what we've got.
W for Wales, who voted to go.
X is the mark your intention to show.
"Y?" is the question that some want to pose -
A Zero-Sum game or a punch on the nose?

"You lost. So, shut up now" some Brexiters say.
"We took back control and we gave it to May."
"And to Parliament?" "No - just May, Davis and Fox;
We campaigned and WE weren't the only ones sinning;
Now Brexit approaches, let's see what we're winning!
So, let's take the money, and open the box."

Cricket Scoreboard

Osborne - hit wicket - 0

Cameron - could not continue - 0

(was thinking of going for 50 but in the end was out for a duck)

Farage - foot in mouth - 0

(never managed a proper innings)

Johnson - caught and bowled Gove - minus 350 million

(This was an unusual dismissal, as he was bowled in the back by a team-mate and then caught out standing at silly mid-off)

Corbyn - has not been in to bat yet, but fighting with his team-mates to stay on the pitch (getting some support from the crowd)

Sturgeon - scoring steadily at the other end but no one is recognising her scores

Crabb - retired hurt - 0

Carney - not out - 1.3

Gove - run out - 0

May and Leadsom are both padding up, who will be next in bat?

Hopefully we'll see some improvement in the UK batting, otherwise the UK will have lost without the other side needing to take the field. A UK follow-on in 2 years' time is a possibility.

Interesting to look back on this. May hit an early 50 without really knowing what she was doing but failed to score after that and eventually was caught out and retired hurt.

2. Article 50

Brexit Cokey

29 November 2016

The question of who could trigger article 50 went to the High Court.

So, it's EU in, it's EU out.
In? Out? In? Out? Debate it all about.
You do the referendum, what a turn around.
Cameron's the first one out.

CHORUS:
Oh, Brexit equals Brexit.
Oh, Brexit equals Brexit.
Oh, Brexit equals Brexit.
Eyes wide, arms out, don't look back.

So which Tories in, and which Tories out?
Boris in, Boris win? No, he's gone straight out.
You do the nominations and you turn around.
Fox, Crabbe and Gove all out.

So, will May get in and edge Leadsom out?
You got to do the voting now to sort the leader out.
You've only just got started and you turn around.
Leadsom has gone straight out.

So, Theresa May is the Brexit Boss.
The naughty boys are put in bat to try and sort it out.

Johnson Fox and Davis have to share the house.
That's what it's all about.

If you want to know just what Brexit is,
Theresa May is just the one to sort out any doubt.
Brexit is what Brexit means and Brexit equals Brexit,
That's what it's all about.

Farage was in but Farage goes out.
Light fight, strife rife, go and sort it out.
Elect another leader, I forgot her name.
She was in, but she's gone straight out.

Mr Corbyn's in, but they want him out.
So, they go all out in a bid to force him out.
And they ask the Party members who first put him in,
And they don't want to put him out.

Now then Scotland's in, but it might go out.
Sturgeon wants to stay, however Scotland's heading out.
If England left the UK then the exit's done,
With the Irish and the Scots not out.

Can the leader leave, can she take us out?
Send them number 50, show what she's about.
Lord Pannick asked the judges, and the judges said,
"Now we will spell it out..."

"....The Executive cannot change the laws.
1688 the Bill of Rights resolved all doubt.
The Commons and the Lords must meet with open doors.
Parliament must sort this out".

Farage didn't want any foreign interference.
He went to say his bit for Trump to try to help him out.
Trump would like him to be ambassador.
That is a very strange shout.

Brexit was to stop the enormous cost,
For 350 million was the weekly going out.
Now the Brexit bill is a bitter pill,
As it's 40 billion to get out.

Single market in, single market out?
It wasn't on the voting paper, so can we go out?
Or is the thing we voted on, constitutionally,
Single market in, but EC out?

Referendums in, and elections out.
Here and there in Europe we'll see voters coming out.
A kaleidoscope, which belied its scope;
When the music stops, we'll turn about.

Is the story done? No, it's just begun.
Voting? Gloating? Or showboating? What's it all about?
"Have your cake and eat it" is what's on the pad.
A can of worms? What will come out?

Single market in? Single market out?
In? Out? In? Out? Debate it all about.
We had the referendum - what a turn around.
What was it all about?

Inspired by: *The Hokey-Cokey*

Remain Lied Too

December 2016

It has been commented that this songbook has so far not really given an equal representation to the Leave campaign arguments. So, let me try to express one of the Leave campaign arguments I have often heard which I find quite intriguing, namely "Remain lied too".

(I have many friends who voted "Leave" and they had their rationale for doing so - this song is not about the voters. but rather about those campaign leaders for whom the cap fits).

You think we told some lies
About the NHS?
We'll own no porky pies,
But someone said that, yes.
They said they'd do it,
And they put it on a bus.
We hoped you'd like it,
But not blame it on us.
Oh yes, we lied, lied, lied,
Led you a ride ride ride,
So, join our side, side, side, side.

Well it's true that our campaign
Showed improvements medically.
How the doctor sees you fast
And we put that on TV.
Until the morning
When enough had voted Leave;

Until the dawning
And the thought that we won't grieve.
Oh yes, we lied, lied, lied,
Led you a ride, ride, ride,
So join our side, side, side, side.

We said that it's ok -
Life outside the old EU-
For Norway Switzerland
And another one or two.
Stuff the Treaty,
And you know where you can park it.
Leave the union,
But stay in the Single Market.
Oh yes, we lied, lied, lied,
Led you a ride, ride, ride,
So, join our side, side, side, side.

Well ok we gave some facts
That were not facts at all.
We told a tale or two,
And some stories that were tall.
But it's ok -
For that wasn't only us;
For Remain did -
Though they didn't have a bus.
Oh yes, we lied, lied, lied,
Led you a ride, ride, ride.
So, join our side, side, side, side.

So, you can ignore our lies
From each whopper to sound-bite.
No more "wherefores" or "why"s,
For two Wrongs make a Right.
Cause Remain lied,
And we'll prove it all to you
They're the blame side
And they said some rubbish too.
Oh yes, we lied, lied, lied,
Led you a ride, ride, ride,
But what about the other side?

They said if we vote leave
Without a plan, that's rash -
Our credit rating heave,
And the currency would crash.
They said the trade deals
Would not follow straight away.
They said you made deals
But it takes many a day.
Oh yes, we lied, lied, lied,
Led you a ride, ride, ride,
But what about the other side?

So, if you'd voted Stay
Then that would have been unfair,
If you worried that your life
On the outside won't compare.
Don't go for their lies
That UK will be a debtor.
So stick with our lies,

And you'll find they are much better.
Oh yes, we lied, lied, lied
Led you a ride, ride, ride,
But what about the other side?

So, I hope you see our lies
Were not unique to us.
Remain were just as bad
Even though they had no bus.
So this you'll give us?
For we really think that's fair.
Will you forgive us?
Though in fact we couldn't care.
Oh yes, we lied, lied, lied,
Led you a ride, ride, ride
But what about the other side?

They warned bad things to come
If we made an EU exit.
Well it hasn't all been done,
Though we haven't yet had Brexit.
And so it's all right.
Nothing else can yet go wrong.
Just wait till midnight -
But that goes beyond this song.
Oh yes, we lied, lied, lied,
Led you a ride, ride, ride
But what about the other side?

Inspired by: *She Loves You*
– with more verses than the original

You're in EU, Going for Exit

26 January 2017

EXCLUSIVE PREVIEW of the expected conversation as Theresa May visits Donald Trump.

Trump:
Your hand, Mrs May, please come in my cage;
I'd like to turn your light on.
Your land, Mrs May, is an empty page
That I would like to write on.

May:
Well, right on!

Trump:
You're in EU, going for exit.
Alarm bells are ringing loud.
If you're the PM, going for Brexit
You'll want to draw a crowd.
Totally unprepared are you,
To play W T O
Truthful and straight and scared are you;
Only one way to go!
You need someone older and madder
Telling you what to do.
You need someone bigger and badder
I'll take care of you.

May:
I'm in EU going for exit
That's what we have to do.
Though I was then with the 48
Leave won with 52.
I need someone older and madder
Telling me what to do.
You are someone bigger and badder
I'll depend on you.

Trump:
I'm a dandy, and I'm quite handy.
Alternative facts are too.
I like torture more than I ought to
I might do some to you.
I like Texaco but I hate Mexico
I'll build a wall, it's true.
Visit my city, I'll grab your treaty
I'll take care of you.

I might call you if I don't wall you,
You'll never have to wait.
I may spook you or maybe nuke you.
My missiles all fly straight.
I can turn the rest into vapour -
NATO, G7, EU
I can sign my name on a paper.
I'll take care of you.

They dance off together round the White House garden.

Inspired by: *You are Sixteen, Going on Seventeen*

Now She Is A Leaver

1 April 2017

Once she thought that Brexit was a fairy-tale,
Then for other people not for her.
UKIP out to get her.
That's the way it seemed.
Disappointment, heartache faced their dreams.
Then she saw the vote;
Now she is a leaver.
There's not a trace
Of doubt in her mind.
She's PM.
Oh, she'll be a leaver
Till she dies.

The EU seemed a reasonable give and take.
It seemed the more we gave the more we got.
Have referendum,
Then the doubts we'll end 'em,
But for various reasons vote was out.
So she saw the vote;
Now she is a leaver.
There's not a trace
Of doubt in her mind.
She's PM
Oh, she'll be a leaver
Till she dies.
So, she saw the vote.
Now she is Theresa.

She doesn't gloat,
Or change her mind.
She is Theresa.
It'll please her
If eu's kind.

Inspired by: *I'm a Believer*

Knowing Me Knowing EU

1 April 2017

Based on her new-found beliefs, Theresa May issued Article 50, more or less as follows:

No more tax-free exports.
No more words from experts.
Got the bill straight through the house
Without a dent.
Then the note with article
Fifty was sent.

Knowing me, knowing eu (ah-haa),
Forty-eight, fifty-two.
Knowing me, knowing eu (ah-haa),
We just have to face it, this time we're through
(This time we're through, time we're through, we're really through).
Breaking treaties with the EC, I know but we have to go
(We have to go this time ,
We have to go, this time we know).
Knowing me, knowing eu,
It's the best we can do.

No more EC orders.
No more easy borders.
In these old familiar places,
Farage would play.
Now there's just two years before
Going away.

Knowing me, knowing eu (ah-haa),
There is nothing we can do.
Knowing me, knowing eu (ah-haa),
We just have to hand the control to eu.
(Control to you, control to you)
This time it's true, we're really through).
Breaking treaties with the EC I know but we have to go.
(We have to go this time
Two years we go, that time I know).
Knowing me, knowing eu,
It's the best we can do.

What I would like, real now.
Cherry pick our deal now.
But you said we can't do that.
That's such a shame.
Now we're got 2 years, that's all.
Who can we blame?
Knowing me, knowing eu (ah-haa),
There is nothing we can do.
Knowing me, knowing eu (ah-haa),
We just have to hand the control to eu,
(Control to you, control to you).
This time it's true, we're really through.
On security I made threats I know, but we have to go
(We have to go this time,
Two years we go, that time I know).
Knowing me, knowing eu,
It's the best we can do.

Inspired by: *Knowing Me, Knowing You*

EU Responds to Article 50.

8 April 2017

Within a few days the EU responded, and this is what they said (roughly speaking)

At first we were not worried, thought you had it planned
Till the Tory party argument got out of hand;
And then they made a crazy fuss upon a bus that was so long,
And no-one heard the experts say this bus was simply wrong.
And so you're out – you've made your case.
I just walked in to find Teresa with her Number Fifty Face.
Your referendum had no lock
Or threshold to make it through,
And so now you've chosen Brexit forty-eight to fifty-two.

Go now go. And shut the door.
Negotiate your trade deals, we won't do them any more.
Weren't you the ones that always said just how you feel?
Well now please do not imagine
You can cherry-pick your deal.
Oh no not now!
That is not how.
As long as you will live,
You're on your own, that's starting now.
We're united twenty-seven.
This may not quite be heaven,
But, according to our shout,
We'd say it's better in than out, hey hey.

So you talked about three hundred fifty millions?
I think you'll find an exit bill in billions.
And you spent so many days just thinking what was your way out.
We used to worry for UK, but now EU goes on without.

Now see EC – running EU.
Dear Britain we are sorry but we'll manage without you.
And so, you felt like having opt-outs,
And you'd argue all the night,
So, we're saving all our treaties for the ones who'll treat us right.

Go now go. And shut the door.
Negotiate your trade deals, we won't do them any more.
Weren't you the ones who said it's better out than in?
Do you think you'll get a better deal?
You really think you'll win?
Oh that's not true.
And now you're through.
You followed Gove and Boris Johnson, and the Nigel Farage crew.
When they have gone away.
You'll have tariffs all to pay
You may survive
But will you thrive?

Inspired by: *I Will Survive*

3. Apologies Due (Election/Trump)

Maggie May

19 May 2017

Theresa May was eager to secure a larger majority so that she could ignore the right wing of the Conservative Party.

There were limited public appearances, but she did reveal on "The One Show" that her husband put out the rubbish bins.

Wake up, Maggie, I think I got manifesto games from you.
It's my election and I really want to be back to rule.
I keep the country in check.
They'll vote for me what the heck.
Oh Maggie I'm much like you
Every day.
You snatched the milk through the squeals,
And now I'll stop school meals.
I'll put up tax and that will really hurt.

The Mail and Sun, when they're in your face, gotta turn the page.
But that don't worry me now, just talk about Living Wage.
I will control the net;
Course you didn't have that yet.
But Maggie I'm much like you
Every day.
You may have got a rebate
But now it is much too late.
Gotta leave EC though that will really hurt.

All I need is majority to do what I like
Then I'll tell Boris it's time he rode his Boris bike.
I'll do this for the nation,
And reduce the immigration
To tens of thousands yes tens of thousands sure.
Tens of thousands and tens of thousands and that's my say
I don't know when and I don't know how but I will one day;
And the firms that need those workers will really hurt.

I suppose I could collect some votes, go back to grammar schools.
I'll expel any ministers who dare to break my rules.
When opportunity knocks
It's time to hunt Liam Fox.
We won't be late but I've got no time to debate.
I've told my husband "That's your bin;
That's a boy-job for you and Corbyn.
Just don't get him talking as that could really hurt".

If the US leader ever wants me to take a jump
I'll say "Yes thank you, how high oh Mr Trump?
I'll hold your hand, you know,
As your friends are letting you go,
But let's sell weapons to anyone with cash".
Oh Maggie you worked with Reagan
And Bush (the Dad, the sane one).
This special relationship won't really hurt.

All I want is strong and stable, that's what I seem.
I'll ask the country to make the vote for Theresa's team.
As long as I am able
I'll be strong and stable

Stable and strong, that's whether I'm right or wrong.
Oh Maggie let's turn us blue
Till 2022
Let's get those votes and show what really hurts.

Oh Maggie you really turn on my light.
Now you kip on while I just turn to the right....,

... (fade into instrumental on Hammond guitar and bass effects)...

Inspired by: *Maggie May*

I Beg My Pardon

23 July 2017

President Trump took to announcing sackings in the White House Rose Garden. He also speculated on pardoning himself for any offences that the Mueller investigation might find that he had committed.

I beg my pardon.

Who will I sack next in the rose garden?
But it's an illusion
That there was Russian government collusion.

When you're me you gotta be
A little tricky, yes you see, so don't blow ho ho ho.

I beg my pardon.
Who will I sack next in the rose garden?

I have promised you some walls, and some other silly banter,
But don't think I'm anything else but a ranter.
I am not your Santa

Well if tweets at half two could all of them come true
Then I would be clear of all accusations,
And same for my relations.
But if we got dirt you shouldn't be hurt,
If there's a leak you gotta take a peek,
And if we are caught you know just what I'll say – eh -

I beg my pardon.
Who will I sack next in the rose garden?
For it's an illusion
That there was Russian government collusion.
I beg my pardon.
Who will I sack next in the rose garden?

You may think that I am fearing a congressional hearing,
But when there is criticism deaf be I,
And I'll sack the head of FBI;
And then there's Sean Spicer - nobody nicer -
But he's going tonight 'cos he didn't say it right.
If you were in my shoes you'd need some fake news,
And if we are caught, you know just what I'll say – eh -

I beg my pardon.
Who will I sack next in the rose garden?
But it's an illusion
That there was Russian government collusion.
I beg my pardon.
Who will I sack next in the rose garden?

Inspired by: *Rose Garden*

4. Brexit Reflections

Brexit Pie

16 November 2017

Long, long time ago,
I can still remember
When the EC used to make me smile.
But I thought if we had a chance
That with a vote we could advance
And maybe we'd be happy for a while.
The campaign was in Wonderland
And what's the news from Sunderland?
I can't remember if I cried
When I saw how much the Leave teams lied
But I knew they were way offside
The day the experts died.
And they were singing
"Bye, bye, to our time with EC.
We are leaving without grieving for the trashed currency."
Them good old boys climb the leadership tree,
Singing "Look what it's doing for me.
Look what it's doing for me."

Did you write the book of Gove?
Did you have faith in Boz above
If his tweets all told you so?
Did you believe he'd rock 'n' roll?
Can bumbling save the nation's soul?
And can you teach me how to bluff and blow?

— Mike Cashman —

Well I know you were in love with him
Because I saw you went out on a limb
You both checked out your brains
In chasing voter gains.
You were a lonely minister in the muck
With a failed career, said "what the pluck"
But you knew you were out of luck
The day the experts died.
And they were singing
"Bye, bye, to our time with EC.
We are leaving without grieving for the trashed currency."
Them good old boys climb the leadership tree,
Singing "Look what it's doing for me.
Look what it's doing for me."

Now, for many years, we'll be on our own,
But you can't build with a single stone,
And that's not how it's meant to be.
Then Theresa spoke to the Tory members
With the Leadsom who no one remembers,
And a vote that's not from you and me.
Oh, and while the Queen was looking down,
Theresa grabbed the primal crown.
The courtroom spoke with force
"Parliament makes the laws".
And while Corbyn read a book on Marx
We did no planning in the dark,
Sent article 50 - what a lark -
The day the experts died.
And they were singing
"Bye, bye, to our time with EC.

We are leaving without grieving for the trashed currency."
Them good old boys climb the leadership tree,
Singing "Look what it's doing for me.
Look what it's doing for me."

Helter skelter in the summer swelter.
June election - what a belter -
10 points high but falling fast.
Theresa's magic money tree
Was used to bribe the DUP;
Let's see how long that will last.
Parliament opened - three hours flat.
The queen she wore her EC hat,
And that's her lucky mascot
To take with her to Ascot.
Negotiations take a while.
Davis did forget his file.
But would we go the extra mile.
The day the experts died?
And they were singing
"Bye, bye, to our time with EC.
We are leaving without grieving for the trashed currency."
Them good old boys climb the leadership tree,
Singing "Look what it's doing for me.
Look what it's doing for me."

Oh, and there we were all in one space.
Negotiations should take place
With no time left to start again.
So come on, Fox be nimble, Davis quick.
Do you think you're wielding a big stick?

Because time is the EC's constant friend.
And as we watched them - not a clue
On transitional deal, or what to do.
The progress now is slow
But where they trying to go?
And as the months tick by with nowt agreed
On Ireland, customs, what we need,
Or citizens, let us take heed,
The day the experts died.
And they were singing
"Bye, bye, to our time with EC.
We are leaving without grieving for the trashed currency."
Them good old boys climb the leadership tree,
Singing "Look what it's doing for me.
Look what it's doing for me."

I saw Theresa sing the blues,
And I asked for some happy news.
She strongly, stably, turned away.
So, I went back to the Leave campaign
Where I'd heard the Brexit joys explained,
But the man there said those pledges wouldn't play.
And while the politicians blundered,
Remainers cried, and Leavers wondered;
Said Davis "How do you feel
If we leave with no Deal?"
Now pledges sound like hollow boasts,
As ministers turned into ghosts,
Resigning one by one their posts,
The day the experts died.
And they were singing

"Bye, bye, to our time with EC.
We are leaving without grieving for the trashed currency."
Them good old boys climb the leadership tree,
Singing "Look what it's doing for me.
Look what it's doing for me."

Inspired by: *American Pie*

When the Nightmare Is Over

1 December 2017

When you're lying awake, with a dismal headache,
And whether you'll sleep, there's no knowing,
And you're vexed by a cough, and the duvet slips off,
And you're worried the way the world's going.
The waiting's inFINite, you hope in a minute
To drop into deep restful slumber;
But the night is half gone, put the radio on,
With sleep timer on some hopeful number.
It plays the world news, and so you hear whose
Adventures spread terrible warning.
It all is depressing, and leaves you still guessing
If sleep's ever coming till morning.

So, ten years ago, there's a night full of woe,
While the pillow I want to unflatten,
And I'm counting the sheep, but I can't get to sleep;
In short, it's the usual pattern.
Well, I get some repose in the form of a dose,
The radio on, and head aching;
But my slumbering teems with such horrible dreams
That I'd very much better be waking.
For I dream that the banks have all run out of francs,
And sterling, and dollars, and ecus;
And people lose millions, and banks all lose billions,
And governments pay for some rescues.

This financial crisis appears to be twice as
Unpleasant as any past failing.
The people of Britain decide that they'll hit on
The government that did the bailing.
For the next thing, it seems, that occurs in my dreams
Is a government by coalition,
That, without temerity, goes for austerity
Taking us all to perdition.

And something quite sinister, for the Prime Minister,
Rumbling deep in his Party,
Some of whom who skip - to party with UKIP -
With sentiments right-wing and hearty.
He thinks that he'll end 'em - with a referendum
That's promised for after election;
His primary mission, one more coalition,
So he'll cite the LibDems rejection
Of that priority – but gets majority,
Unplanned, unwelcome and troubling!
And in the dream now, there's a terrible row -
Discontent with the status quo bubbling.

Seems Boris can't know which way he will go,
But on balance he favours us leaving.
So many MPs making desperate pleas -
I think they'll be Dominic Grieving.
But what's the position of the Opposition?
They advocate staying; they mean it?
But the Leaving campaign then decide to explain
With a sign on a bus; we've all seen it.

There's a dreadful mirage; no, it's Nigel Farage,
And a poster that's frankly quite shocking.
He thinks that he bossed it, and finally lost it;
We see that a snook he is cocking.
Well Cameron's gone, and he's singing a song,
And somebody has to take charge;
At the end of the day, then Theresa may
That's better than Nigel Farage
To fix up our exit; so, Brexit means Brexit,
And now you know as much as they know -
Discussions protracted, as they're all distracted,
Guessing will Theresa May go?

And we're stuck in a mess, though I know we said yes,
And the bill is too large, and that's not a mirage;
And though this is my land, I'm worried for Ireland,
And everyone's tweety, but we have no treaty,
And now I've a headful of problems so dreadful;
You know how it seems, in the craziest dreams.
I've a headache intense and a general sense
That I've crashed on the white cliffs of Dover;
But the darkness has passed, and it's daylight at last,
And the nightmare's been long - ditto, ditto my song -
And thank goodness they're both of them over!

Inspired by: *Lord Chancellor's Song* from "Iolanthe"

Say Goodbye Our Former Partner

December 2017

Say goodbye our former partner,
Let's negotiate in song;
As we still recall percentage -
Fifty-two who want us gone.

Worked all night, our two hearts beating,
Did Phase One, by break of day.
But the joys of deal are fleeting
For Michel and T'resa May.

In the Parliaments they'll judge it;
Is the government afloat?
While she'd dearly like to fudge it,
Her colleagues demand a vote.

Fifty billion we must pay this;
Our reactions are quite mixed.
Please ignore our David Davis,
And pretend that Ireland's fixed.

This is all a big investment;
Hope that no-one harbours doubt.
Not for us, impact assessment;
Let's just see how it turns out.

Every problem, now we'll park it;
Hope the issues won't be seen.

Please don't mention Single Market
Until March, 2019.
Please don't mention Single Market
Until March, 2019.

Inspired by: *When the Carnival is Over*

Where Have All of UKIP Gone?

22 January 2018

Where have all of UKIP gone, all resigning?
Where have all of UKIP gone, all gone away?
Where have all of UKIP gone?
They've disagreed, like everyone.
Oh, when will they ever learn?
Oh, when will they ever learn?

Where have all their leaders gone, all resigning?
Where have all their leaders gone, no-one will last.
Where have all their leaders gone?
They've failed their members, every one.
Oh, when will they ever learn?
Oh, when will they ever learn?

Where have all their ideas gone, if they had any?
Where have all the ideas gone, there's nothing left!
Where have all the ideas gone?
Recycled for the Tory con.
Oh, when will they ever learn?
Oh, when will they ever learn?

Where has Nigel Farage gone, long time passing?
Where has Nigel Farage gone, so do we know?
Where has Nigel Farage gone?
He's on his Euro pension.
Oh, when will we ever learn?
Oh, when will we ever learn?

Inspired by: *Where Have All the Flowers Gone?*

Could We Start Again Please?

6 March 2018

We've been living in EU.
Arguing with EU, but it shouldn't end like this.
This was unexpected,
What do we do now?
Could we start again please?

I've been very hopeful, one time.
Now in the worst way, I think we're going wrong.
Hurry up and tell me,
This is just a dream.
Oh, could we start again please?

I think you've made your point now.
You've even gone a bit too far to get the message home.
Before it gets too frightening,
We ought to call a vote,
So, could we start again please?
(Repeat 5 times)

Adapted from: *Could We start Again, Please*
(Jesus Christ Superstar).

5. More Brexit Realities

Don't Cry for Leave Now, Theresa

7 March 2018

Don't cry for Leave now, Theresa.
The truth is, that if we left "eu",
All through the wild claims,
Their blind insistence,
They kept no promise;
You kept your distance.

It wasn't easy, they thought it strange,
When you tried to explain why to Leave -
That you still need the votes after all that you'd done;
Would they believe you?
All they can see is the Home Sec they once knew,
Although in brown pants and not blue,
A careful precaution for you.

You had to let it happen,
You had to change;
Couldn't stay all your life as Remain.
You'd be out of the Cabinet -
Political exit.
So, you chose Brexit.
Running the show, and Brexit means Brexit.
But nothing impressed them at all.
You ever expected it to?

[Chorus:]
Don't cry for Leave now, Theresa.

The truth is, that if we left "eu",
All through the wild claims,
Their blind insistence,
They kept no promise;
You kept your distance.

And on free tariffs, and on free trade,
You never expected to win.
Though it seemed to Club Leave
We'd have all we desired.
They are illusions.
There aren't the solutions they promised to be.
The answer was here all the time -
So much hurt for our economy
[Chorus:]
Don't cry for Leave now, Theresa.
The truth is, that if we left "eu",
All through the wild claims,
Their blind insistence,
They kept no promise;
You kept your distance.

Have I said too much?
There's nothing much that we are meant to say to you;
For we recognise we are only 48,
And you're the 52.

Inspired by: *Don't Cry for Me, Argentina*

Brexit Mia

28 March 2018

Theresa May admits Brexit is IMPOSSIBLE
  "*Theresa May officially acknowledged that Brexit in the form it was sold to the British people by senior members of her Cabinet – including Boris Johnson, Michael Gove, David Davis and Liam Fox – is simply impossible to deliver.*"
  "*As the leaders of the official Vote Leave campaign, these people promised the UK would get most of the benefits of EU membership outside of the club without bearing the costs or the obligations. May finally came clean on this dishonesty, saying: 'How could the EU's structure of rights and obligations be sustained, if the UK – or any country – were allowed to enjoy all the benefits without all of the obligations?'*"

We been cheated by you, since you know when.
Will we make up our mind, it must come to an end?
Look at us now, will we ever learn?
I don't know how, we're supposed to take back control.
There was cheating before the poll.
Just one bus - three-fifty million sum;
TV ads said the same, so that votes come.
Tory tears, will you flow again?
My, my, how can you complete this?
Tory tears, here you go again.
My, my, couldn't we delete this?

Yes, we've been often quoted,
Sad, since the day we voted.

— *Mike Cashman* —

Why, why, did we ever vote for who?
Tory tears, now we're really though.
My my, we must never vote for you.

I've been angry and sad and I've never been sicker
Now we've heard of the cheat- Cambridge Annal It Icker.
And when we go, when we leave EU
I think you know, that things will look pretty blue.

Just one bus - three-fifty million sum.
TV ads said the same so that votes come.
Tory tears, will you flow again?
My, my, how can you complete this?
Tory tears, here you go again.
My, my, couldn't we delete this?

Inspired by: *Mama Mia*

The Brexit Game

30 May 2018

This is expected to be a best-selling game in the shops this Christmas

1. No experts can play.
2. The players all vote "Yes" or "No" on the rules of the game. The implications of this vote will not become clear until the end of the game.
3. Half of those who voted "Yes" leave the room.
4. All remaining players change places.
5. Whoever can first say "Brexit equals Brexit" leads.
6. The leader waits for 8 months and then issues Article 50.
7. The implementation date for Article 50 is a long way off. So, there is nothing much that needs to be done for a long time now, so you may as well have a general vote. Ignore the outcome.
8. Have a little chat about the question "When is a customs union not a customs union?".
9. What happens next depends whether anyone notices that there are only 9 rounds left until the deadline. You may either have Complacency or Panic.
10. Anyone who has got one can play a Backstop. A Backstop means that you can treat the game as a draw, but the game goes on with uncertain outcomes for everyone else.
11. If you are the leader, you don't actually need to have a Backstop to play a Backstop. Just play it anyway.
12. A Backstop can be overruled by a Backstop for a Backstop. And so on.
13. Players may opt to threaten not to pay.

14. Any players who have disgraced themselves must leave the game. (This rule is waived for anyone with the surname "Johnson").

15. What happens after that? No-one has the foggiest idea. Hopefully it will all be worked out by Christmas. Or the Tooth Fairy.

Round - Like a Brexit Without Exit

7 June 2018

Round - Like a Brexit without exit,
Like a spin without a win,
Like some talks are never ending,
Though they don't seem to begin,
Like some plans that still seem rotten,
That will not do much for us,
Like a promise that's forgotten,
That was written on a bus,
Like a platform that is burning,
Though there's no-one can say why,
Like a calendar that's turning,
As the days and months slip by,
Like the self-defeating exit
Of the unplanned unknown Brexit.

Like a pot without a shaper,
Like the cream without the clot,
Like a mythical White Paper,
Like a team that's lost the plot.
Like a dealer who is shifty,
Who is hiding in a hole,
Since they sent article fifty,
And they gave away control.
Like a platform that is burning,
Though there's no-one can say why,
Like a calendar that's turning,
As the days and months slip by,

Like the self-defeating exit
Of the unplanned unknown Brexit.

Slogans jingle in the memory:
Words that jangle in your head.
How did two years go so quickly?
Was it something that we said?
Labour walks around the issues
Like a noted also-ran.
While the Tory power misuse
Is in office with no plan.
Like the papers fill their pages,
As if progress has been made.
Like she's bought off David Davis,
As the backstop's been portrayed.
Like a crazy hopeful saviour -
That is Boris with the hump;
Like his latest misbehaviour
Is to hand it all to Trump.
When we see that it's all over,
When we wonder what was meant,
For a moment we will not recall
The spring of discontent.

As the talks falter and fall,
See enthusiasm pall.
We did not need this at all.

Inspired by: *Windmills of Your Mind.*

6. World Cup Fever
This Time

15 June 2018

For those who remember the determination of the 1982 England World Cup squad to put all the poor performances behind them and make a proper attempt, which they expressed in song:

This time, more than any other time, this time,
We're going to find a way,
Find a way to get away,
This time, getting Brexit together.
To win a deal
It's what we will set out to do.
We have a dream
Though who else shares it too?

This time, more than any other time, this time,
We're going to fix our trade,
Find a way with our debts paid,
This time, getting Brexit together
We'll get it right.
This time, get it right.
This time
It makes you wonder,
You have to feel,
Why leave the EU
With no good deal?

As we're marching.
On towards who know what?
We leave. Oh Grieve,
We're on our way,
We are Theresa's crew.
Hear the noise
As all of us argue.
This time, more than any other time, this time,
For Ireland there must be a way,
Or a backstop anyway,
This time, getting Brexit together,
We'll get it right.
This time, we'll get it right.

Inspired by: *This Time*

Brexit's Coming Home (Three Lines on the Whip)

3 July 2018

It's coming home. It's coming home. It's coming.
Brexit's coming home.
It's coming home. It's coming home. It's coming.
Brexit's coming home.

Everyone seems to know the score.
They've said it all before.
They just know.
They're so sure.
That we are gonna
Throw it away,
Gonna have no payday,
It's Theresa she may,
'Cos I remember
Three lines from the Whip,
Tory gang succumbing,
We can't blame UKIP,
Cameron saw this coming,

So many lies, so many hawks,
But all those ministers' walks
Wear you down
Through the talks,
But I still see that
Treaty we had,
And a tariff-free zone ,
And the customs were done,

With Customs Union
And a Single Market.

Three lines from the Whip,
Tory gang showboating,
We can't blame UKIP.
What about the voting?
I know that was then.
But it could be again.

Three lines from the Whip,
Back this crazy caper.
We can't blame UKIP
Theresa wants White Paper.   (It's coming home).
Three lines from the Whip. (It's coming home). (It's coming).
Experts are forgetting.
(Brexit's coming home). (It's coming home).
Though some goods we'll ship. (It's coming home). (It's coming).
No good deal we're getting.
(Brexit's coming home). (It's coming home).
Three lines from the Whip. (It's coming home). (It's coming).
They try to keep order.
(Brexit's coming home). (It's coming home).
Think we made a slip, (It's coming home). (It's coming).
On the Irish border. (Brexit's coming home). (It's coming home).
Three lines from the Whip. (It's coming home). (It's coming).
No good deal we're writing.
(Brexit's coming home). (It's coming home).
Watching our pounds dip. (It's coming home). (It's coming).
Tories still are fighting. (Brexit's coming home).
Repeat until March 2019

Inspired by: *Football's Coming Home.*

Once More onto the Pitch, Dear Friends, Once More

5 July 2018

FOR ENGLAND IN THE WORLD CUP

Once more onto the pitch, dear friends, once more,
Or close up the wall for that side's free kick.
In play there's nothing so becomes a team
As good possession and goal chances quick,
But if the opposition butt with heads,
Or other action meant to do you harm,
Then summon up your greatest self-control -
Disguise your nature with an icy calm.

Imitate the action of the Gareth -
He of the South Gate, with waistcoat blue.
He knows full well vict'ry and heartache
As you would if 'twas done to you.
So, take your corners Trippier with precision.
Locate the heads of Stones and then of Kane,
That he should flick into the gaping net,
If was not tackled in a way insane.

Avoid the cards of yellow and of red;
You are more worthy than to deal in those.
Avoid the men of yellow; seek the red
Unless to tackle yellow-shirted foes.

The shots from far and near give hope of goal,
And now the crowd encourage with a roar.

The ninety minutes serve us well, but still,
I see you're up for penalties once more
If it should come to that. The game's afoot!
The V A R shows things not as they seem.
Follow your captain; and upon this charge
Cry - God for Harry! England, and the Queen.

Inspired by: Henry V speech, before Harfleur,
"Once more unto the breach dear friends once more"
Henry V, Act 3. Scene 1

7. Heck it's Chequers – and Trump

19th Brexit Breakdown

9 July 2018

(To David Davis)

You're the kind of person you meet at negotiation parties.
You got some votes, but got no notes, this isn't where
your heart is.
Well it seems to be that you've not done much within that
two long years.
And though you've tried you just can't hide you haven't
solved our fears.
You better stop, look around.
Here it comes, here it comes, here it comes, here it comes.
Here comes your nineteenth Brexit breakdown.

(To Boris Johnson)
When you were Mayor you were treated fair,
But you thought you would deceive.
Your right to remain was very plain, but then you fancied Leave.
You made some promises back then, and never did repent.
But she kept you in as Foreign Sec, to keep inside the tent.
You better stop, look around.
Here it comes, here it comes, here it comes, here it comes.
Here comes your nineteenth Brexit breakdown.
Oh, who's to blame, this plan's just insane.
Well, nothing you do don't seem to work.
It only seems to make the matters worse.
Oh, please.

You were still with Gove when he gave that shove, which really messed your mind;
So, you weren't Prime Minister that day, and you thought that was unkind.
And you've sort of done some job since then, if we don't hear what you say.
But we really need a grown-up voice to speak for us today.
You better stop, look around.
Here it comes, here it comes, here it comes, here it comes.
Here comes your nineteenth Brexit breakdown.
Oh, who's to blame, this plan's just insane.
Well, nothing you do don't seem to work.
It only seems to make the matters worse.
Oh, please.

Inspired by: *19th Nervous Breakdown.*

Trumpet So Wide

13 July 2018

After Trump's visit to the UK

Think I'm gonna be glad,
I think it's today, yeah.
The Trump that's driving me mad
Is going away.
He's got a ticket to ride.
He knows that he'd better hide.
He knows how often he lied,
And he don't care.

He said our re-lationship
Was special and large.
He said he thought that BoJo
Could well be in charge.
He's got a trumpet so wide.
He knows that he'd better hide.
He knows how often he lied,
And he don't care.

I don't know why he's flying so high,
He ought to think twice,
Review his ad-vice, from now.
Before he gets to saying goodbye,
He ought to confess,
He ought to tweet less, from now.

Think I'm gonna be glad,
I think it's today, yeah.
The Trump that's driving me mad
Is going away.
He's got a trumpet so wide.
He thinks that Putin's onside.
He knows how often he lied,
And he don't care.

Inspired by: *Ticket to Ride*

It's My Brexit and I'll Cry if I Want to

25 July 2018

A little song for Theresa to sing after the Chequers weekend

It's my Brexit and I'll cry if I want to.
Why can't we hold it,
And Take Back Control it?
You will cry too, when it happens to you.

Everyone knows where my Boris has gone,
And David left the same time.
Why was he dissing the Deal
When he's supposed to be mine?

It's my Brexit and I'll cry if I want to.
Why can't we hold it,
And Take Back Control it?
You will cry too, when it happens to you.

Inspired by: *It's My Party and I'll Cry if I Want To*

I'm Just A Girl Who Cain't Say "Go"

27 July 2018

It ain't so much a question of not knowin' what to do;
It ain't so flippin tricky to explain.
I've heerd a lot of experts and think some of them are true,
I've know'd we do much better with Remain,
And nonsense that I'm talking, don't believe,
'Cos put me into office – I'll say Leave.

I'm jist a girl who cain't say "Go",
I'm in a terrible fix.
I always think our plan we'll show
Just when the Deal's got no ticks.
When a Rees-Mogg tries to hold me tight,
I know I orta give his face a smack.
But as soon as he amends my Bill,
I somehow, sorta want amend him back!

I'm jist a fool when Trump is here -
Hold hands, like we're in a plot.
I asked the Queen - have him shot.
How c'n I be what I'm not?
I cain't say "Go"!

Whut you goin' to do when a Gove gets smarty, and starts
to talk "Party"
Whut you goin' to do?
S'posing 'at he says that he's got a mandate, a can-date, a
plan-date,

Whut you goin' to do?
S'posin' 'at he says 'at the Deal's on order,
And he don't worry 'bout the Irish border.
Whut you goin' to do when he talks that way?
Be a hoarder?

I'm jist a girl who cain't say "Go",
Leaving's a horrible meal.
With or without a plan to show -
Giving up hope of a Deal.
I'd like to think we are a catch -
But that don't seem to convince anyone.
Every time I try a Brussels match,
I have a funny feeling that they won.
Although I can see all the head lines
I give up all my red lines
Because we hit the deadlines
And I see dangerous signs,
I caint say "Go".

Inspired by: *I'm Just a Girl who Caint Say "No"*
– from "Oklahoma"

How Do You Solve A Problem Like Our Brexit?

3 August 2018

She says that Brexit equals Brexit -
Makes no sense to me.
She holds elections, doesn't win,
And bribes the DUP.
And underneath her Brexit
All the weaknesses she'll see.
I know why Cam'ron's singing on his exit.

We're losing ways to work as one.
They want us to get real.
We're always late for everything.
We're heading for "No Deal".
I hate to have to say it,
But I very firmly feel,
That Brexit's not an asset to our country.

"I'd like to say a word on his behalf".
("Then say it, Environmental Secretary")
"Well, Boris makes me laugh".
(All titter).

How do you solve a problem like our Brexit?
How is it we have made this mess unique?
How do you solve a problem like our Brexit?
And save 350 million per week?

Many a thing the twenty-seven tell us,
And we think they think we think they are fools

But how is it we can stay,
When this is what we will say:
"We'd like to leave the club and change the rules."
Oh, how do you solve a problem like our Brexit?
How do you hold a pipedream in your hand?

Now on Brexit I'm confused,
Out of focus and bemused,
Things are never quite exactly they seem.
And she'll say to her guys "Go, deal"
And start hoarding for a "No Deal",
It's a drama! It's a nightmare! It's a dream!
We'll increase our Customs fees,
Drive the City overseas,
It will throw the Irish border in a mess,
And the lorries that we sent
Will be parked all over Kent,
It's a headache! It's a Farage!
Let's confess!

How do you solve a problem like our Brexit?
How do you find a plan and pin it down?
How do you get some answers on the Brexit?
From a fantasist! A Gove-o'-the wisp! A clown!
Deals with others will be taking longer,
Trade with Europe we will not enhance,
But here's what we'll achieve,
If we choose to Leave -
Our passports will be blue! (though made in France).
Oh, how do you solve a problem like our Brexit?
How do you hold a pipedream in your hand?

Inspired by: *How do you solve a problem like Maria?*

Whatever Happened to The Brexit Deal?

18 August 2018

Oh what happened to y'eu?
Whatever happened to us?
What became of the people
Who chose the bus?
Two years is almost over -
The time went by so fast
And with no deal we look forward to
A false past.

There was a time when truth didn't matter,
Only the votes to gain.
And lying and cheating were both
Part of the Leave Campaign.
"Never look back" they told us,
"Cos we're the 52."
"We will know what we're doing".
"Leaving the EU".

Oh, what happened to y'eu?
Whatever happened to us?
What became of the people
Who chose the bus?
Two years is almost over -
The time went by so fast.
And the only thing to look forward to
Is the past.

We see ministers in a fools' paradise,
Looking for a sunny day.
Waiting with their head in the clouds,
Hoping Ireland goes away.
"No deal's better than a bad deal,"
Those were the words they said.
There's a different sort of lying now that
They've not made the bed.

Oh, what happened to y'eu?
Whatever happened to us?
What became of the people
Who chose the bus?
Two years is almost over -
The time went by so fast.
And the only thing to look forward to
Is the past.

Oh, what happened to y'eu?
Whatever happened to us?
What became of the people
Who chose the bus?

Inspired by: *Oh, What Happened to You?*
Theme from *"Whatever Happened to the Likely Lads?"*

8. Preparing to Leave Port-A-Loo

14 September 2018

Worried about no-deal Brexit? The government has made preparations, by ordering port-a-loos to line the M20 motorway once the lorry backlog builds up.

My, my, with Port-a-loo Theresa May did surrender.
Oh yeah, and we have met our destiny in quite a similar way.
The Brexit deal that can't be done
Won't have us all on the run.
Port-a-loo - M20 line up, along the way;
Port-a-loo - khazis for drivers on motorway;
Port-a-loo - no deal gridlock, so loos are sent;
Port-a-loo - stretching the toilets out over Kent;
Port-a-loo - Finally facing our Port-a-loo.

My, my, we tried to get a deal but we were wronger,
Oh yeah, and now it seems our only chance is giving up the fight.
And how could we ever refuse
If they lay out so many loos.
Port-a-loo - never mind no deal, we are not sore.
Port-a-loo - Promise to use them for ever more.
Port-a-loo - Plastic bogs there if you wanted to.
Port-a-loo - Stuck on the road but we still poo.
Port-a-loo - Finally facing our Port-a-loo.
And how could we ever refuse
If they lay out so many loos.

Port-a-loo - Couldn't escape if I wanted to.
Port-a-loo - Brexit is taking us into you.
Port-a-loo - Finally facing our Port-a-loo.

Inspired by: *Waterloo*

9. Results of the Cluster-Interaction

Brexit's a Trick, not a Treat?

31 October 2018

If you hoped for a Brexit that's sweet
As a cake you can have and can eat,
Do you now realise
The extent of the lies,
And that Brexit's a trick, not a treat?

Doh, We're Here

13 November 2018

Doh, we're here, we are still here.
Ray of light, first in a while?
May, is done? Well not so far.
Raab, now Britain is an isle.
So, what's next for heaven's sake?
La-La-Land is this whole show.
Tea, and have and eat the cake?
Which will bring us back to Doh Doh Doh Doh Doh

Inspired by: *Doe, a Deer*

Rock Paper Scissors

14 November 2018

SENSE WARNING: There is a serious point in this one ....

If Brexit plans meet no-one's wishes,
Concerning trade, borders, and fishes,
Let Rock be Remain,
Deal is Paper - that's plain,
And Leave with No Deal must be scissors.

With single transferable vote,
And "Scissors cuts paper " - straight quote,
When the votes are all penned,
And transferred in the end.
Scissors loses to Rock as you'll note.

And what this quick process can show
Is that if all who voted to Go
Have to choose one thing plain,
To compare with Remain,
Then the Leavers might lose, you may know.

Now look at that old vote again.
The insight from this we may gain,
With three boxes to fill,
Then the People's true Will
Might pick no option versus Remain.

So don't call this clever or tactical,
And it wouldn't be undemocratical.
Now the three ways are clearer,
To find which are dearer,
To voters - let's check this, be practical.

10. Theresa May Battles On
Oh, Theresa First Looked Out

12 December 2018

A seasonal song now that the parliamentary vote on the deal is postponed

Oh, Theresa first looked out
On the referendum.
Forty years of Tory doubts –
David thought he'd end 'em.
But six years of swingeing cuts –
How the mem'ry lingers.
Fifty-two, no "ifs" no "buts",
Gave the lad two fingers.

Well the Leavers showed how they
Were so skilled at leaving.
All soon left the field of fray,
It's beyond believing.
So, Theresa was alone,
And went to the palace.
"Please, Oh Queen, I'm on my own.
Pass the poisoned Chalice".

Two years on and not much done -
She's afraid of wreckers.
"Seems to me, no deal yet won.
Sort it out at Chequers.
Don't you dare resign and jeer -

Or you'll lose your gofers,
And the cars that brought you here,
And your pricey chauffeurs."

David Davis took no heed.
Wrote a little letter.
Boris read what he'd agreed.
Thought he could do better.
So much for the Leaver gang,
Mrs May got Raab in
Loyalty was her demand
To protect from Corbyn.

"We will set up such a deal
We'll have our own tax top".
"Yes, if that's the way you feel.
But you'll need a backstop.
That is the insurance plan
Before bonds we sever.
You just cannot kick the can
Down the road for ever."

Well you know what happens next.
Boris loudly rages.
Raab, Davis and Mogg are vexed.
At five eight five pages.
"Oh, dear me, we're not done yet."
Is the exclamation.
"It's crucial we also get
Future declaration".

Brexiteers don't like the plan.
Nor do the Remainers.
MPs diss it all they can;
Say her faults are heinous.
Though she says she's taking note.
"You are such a jerk – oh
You should really have a vote"
Says the Speaker Bercow.

Though Theresa's had enough
There is no abatement
Of the questions which are tough
On her sudden statement.
"I can't stand these rebel bands,
These MPs complaining.
Think I'll go to Netherlands,
As I hate Remaining".

One six four have had their say,
Many more intending.
Will they talk another day?
Is this never ending?
If we have a different game,
Debate we'll again use,
If the deal is just the same,
The debate continues.

"If you're voicing all these doubts,
How else would you end 'em?"
Some have said to Mrs May.
"Final referendum."

"No, I'm stable and I'm strong.
That dice I will not throw.
What if they should get it wrong
Like they did two years ago?"

"Bring me votes and bring me tweets;
I will not be gloomy.
We have just three one six seats,
One five nine will do me.
Heck knows how I'll manage then -
Parliament can be blowed.
They can all applaud me when
I kick the can right down the road."

Inspired by: *Good King Wenceslas*

The First No Deal

19 December 2018

The first "No Deal" that Theresa said then
Was to certain poor ministers in Number 10;
To ministers who didn't know what or how
But agreed with contingency spending for now.
No Deal, No Deal, and conceal what you feel.
Let's spend 4 billion so they think it's real.

The ministers looked, and beheld a great vote,
Which had happened two years ago, and they took note,
And to the group it seemed that they had
A mandate to continue in good times and bad.
No Deal, No Deal, and conceal what you feel.
Let's spend 4 billion so they think it's real.

And by the light of that same vote,
Five eight five pages - agreement were wrote.
To have an agreement was their intent,
But the idea went tits-up in Parliament.
No Deal, No Deal, and conceal what you feel.
Let's spend 4 billion so they think it's real.

They thought that the vote must be their way,
And they said we must fall in behind Mrs May.
But now, they were stuck, even though they followed;
Decisively, they kicked the can down the road.
No Deal, No Deal, and conceal what you feel.
Let's spend 4 billion so they think it's real.

We like some votes, but we do like to choose
Whether to vote or not, just because we might lose.
We prefer to avoid our plan being assessed.
Because everyone might see it's not quite the best.
No Deal, No Deal, and conceal what you feel.
Let's spend 4 billion so they think it's real.

We'll do, they said, what the people have sought;
So, the people's rejoicing will be our first thought.
Some troops should be there, on stand-by in case
The rejoicing's in danger of swamping the place.
No Deal, No Deal, and conceal what you feel.
Let's spend 4 billion so they think it's real.

Inspired by: *The First Noel*

Dance for the Deal

31 December 2018

Chris Grayling arranged a deal with a ferry company with no ships and no track record.

I have many times been involved in Due Diligence exercises. Fascinated to see that the government has undertaken Due Diligence on the operation of a company that has no operation

Dance for the deal.
Your ships aren't real.
Dance for the deal.
Though no boats come in.

You shall have a contract,
Though the ships we've none tracked.
You shall have a contract,
Though no boats come in.

Well what is the difference,
We have done due diligence.
Well what is the difference
Though no boats come in.

There's no cancellations,
And no aberrations.
Check no deviations,
When no boats come in.

Here is fourteen million.
We must spend four billion.
Here is fourteen million,
Though no boats come in.

We have looked at your site,
Full of lies - a poor site,
You set up with foresight.
Though no boats come in.

Dance for the deal.
Your ships aren't real.
Dance for the deal,
Though no boats come in.

Inspired by *"Dance for Your Daddy" (When the Boat Comes In)*

They Said There'll Be Deals at Brexit.

They said there'll be deals at Brexit.
They said there'll be new tax stop.
But instead they just kept on talking,
Now rejecting their own backstop.
I remember the June vote morning,
Lies on a bus denied when they won,
And the crash of the pound, with no happy rebound,
And the damage then already done.

They sold us a dream of Brexit.
Sunderland votes came in that night.
As we heard then a fairy story,
To build belief in this total sugar.
Nissan believed in Good-Deal Brexit,
With sixty million to bring them onside,
'till it went down the pan and they cancelled the plan.
Even bribes may not work when you lied.

I believe in a No-Deal Brexit.
Let's have hope for our future life.
We will cope with no winter lettuce.
We'll have troops to control the strife.
They said there'll be boats at Brexit.
They said that the fruit can curve.
It's planned so well, be it heaven or hell.
The Brexit you get you deserve.

Inspired by: *They Said There'll Be Snow at Christmas*

You're Got Brexit, Needing an Exit

So, concerning the Deal that the Government negotiated and proposed and that the Prime Minster said could not be changed and the EU said could not be changed because that would violate an international peace treaty:

*   - There has been a decisive vote against that Deal*

*   - The vote was initiated by a back-bencher but supported by the Government, who voted for the amendment, and hence voted against their own proposal.*

You're got Brexit, needing an exit,
Unsure of what to do.
Booking non-boats now, losing your votes now,
Sad with just two-oh-two.
You want tax stop, but your old backstop
Just got thumbs down, it's true.
You need authority with a majority
Who'll back a way that's new.

Leave trade quotas, we are the voters
With an idea or two.
You think we're outers, forgot about us,
But there is a way through.
You get your best Deal, then see how we feel,
Cos when we know what's true
Although you messed up, if you confessed up,
Voting could work for you.

Inspired by: *You are Sixteen, Going on Seventeen*

Take a Chance on Me.

There was speculation about Jeremey Corbyn working with Theresa May
        JEREMY CORBYN'S RESPONSE IN FULL:

If you change your mind, I'm the first in line.
Theresa I'm still free;
Work with Jeremy.
If you need me, let me know,
gonna be around.
All you've got to do, is put "No Deal " down.

If you're all alone, when the Tory votes have flown,
Theresa I'm still free,
Take a chance on me.
I'll keep off the People's Vote, and this ain't no lie,
Does that float your boat, will you let me try?
Take a chance on me.
(That's all I ask of you Theresa)
Take a chance on me.

We can start bending, we can stop spending, as long as we're together.
Stop the ferry contract, that should be ending, there's no case of "whether".
'Cos you know I've got
So much that I wanna do, when I dream I've got the job from you,
It's magic.
You want me to leave it there,

Don't want a Labour affair,
But I think you know
That I can't let go.

Now you talked Remain, worked with their campaign,
But you were a pain, and you boosted Leave.
If you like both, I get that,
gotta keep in play.
If the fence is where you're sat,
Then that's where I stay.

You were all alone when the Leadsom's flown;
Gove and Boris they
Shot themselves that day.
Gonna hope for very best, just as you found then.
Hope the foes will all go west, leave us number ten.

Take a chance on me.
(Come on, give me a turn, will you?)
Take a chance on me.
Oh, you can take your time Theresa,
I'm in no hurry, for your deselection.
You don't wanna hurt me, Theresa,
Don't worry, I'll win election.
My votes are strong enough to last when things are rough.
And tragic.
You say that I waste my time but I can't get this off my mind.

Now let's talk some sense.
Let me on your fence,
If you change your mind, I'm the first in line,

Theresa I'm still free.
Work with Jeremy.
If you need me, let me know, gonna be around.
All you have to do, is to put "no Deal" down.

If you're all alone when the Tory votes have flown,
Theresa I'm still free.
Take a chance on me.
Gonna do my very best, Theresa can't you see, yes.
Gotta put me to the test, take a chance on me.
(Take a chance, take a chance, take a chance on me).

Inspired by: *Take a Chance on Me*

11. The last days of Theresa May

The Many Votes of Brexit

For the first vote of Brexit, Theresa said there'd be
Withdrawal from the EC.
For the second vote of Brexit, Theresa said there'd be
Words on the backstop,
And withdrawal from the EC.
For the third vote of Brexit, Theresa said there'd be
Her resignation,
Words on the backstop,
And withdrawal from the EC.
For the fourth vote of Brexit, Theresa said there'd be
Talks with the Corbyn,
Her resignation,
Words on the backstop,
And withdrawal from the EC.
For the fifth vote of Brexit, Theresa said there'd be
More Commons votes;
Talks with the Corbyn,
Her resignation,
Words on the backstop,
And withdrawal from the EC.
To be continued…. possibly leading to…
For the 12th vote of Brexit, Theresa said there'd be
General election,
No referendum,
No more petitions,
More tries at whipping,

Euro elections,
No Customs Union
One more extension,
More Commons votes.
Talks with the Corbyn,
Her resignation,
Words on the backstop,
And withdrawal from the EC.

Inspired by: *Twelve Days of Christmas*

Menu for EU Summit Dinner

Cocktails on Therese

Starmers:
- On Toast
- In the soup

(Crudités a la Mark Francois were offered, but nobody wanted them)

Main Courbyns:
- Cold Turkey
- Ham on d'bone
- Irish Stew
- L'éléphant a la Chambre
- Whales Divided
- Pommes d'Angleterre *
- String-along-Beans

* will be taken out of the room part way through

Desserted Figures:
- Sweet Nothings
- Choice of Fudge
- Hard Cheese-Mogg
- Sour Grapes

(Eton Mess is not available at this summit because the relevant chef is indisposed, but he hopes to bring this dish back next time).

To drink:
- Vintage Whine
- Scotch Whimsy
- Any Port in a Storm

Then: the Bill (Cash)
Diners said they only want to stay at the table until 11.30 pm
Extended to 12.15 by special request.
Revised to 1 a.m. as long as they plan to go to bed at some definite time.
Amended - they can stay until 2 a.m. if they help with the washing-up.
Finally - we give up, you're never going, are you?

Sit on the Fence

Mr Corbyn, dear ladies and gents,
Has decided what he thinks makes sense.
While you may want to note
If he'd like you to Vote,
Instead he'll still sit on the fence.

Final Say

8th May 2019

Liverpool and Spurs prove that, ultimately, it's possible to stay in Europe even when the initial results suggest the opposite. Nothing is decided until everything is decided. The players have had the #FinalSay.

This wouldn't have been achieved without the significant contributions from immigrants however.

Initial results were adverse.
They really could not be much worse.
But continue to play
Until #FinalSay
For Liverpool, Britain and Spurs.

I Might as Well Reign until September.

Theresa May under pressure to resign
BREAKING NEWS - PM STANCE FOR FRIDAY'S MEETING.

Of course, I know I only had one job to do;
I thought I'd spin it out till 2022.
But I've heard bad news from the 1922,
So, I might as well reign until September.

I take on Parliament, the place where my plan wrecks.
But I look forward to my future Brexit Secs.
To MV4,5,6 and what I might do next,
So, I might as well reign until September.

Manchester Conference will be my future chance.
Don't give me negative votes - "don't"s and "won't"s and "can't"s.
Just let me stay to show my strong and stable dance.
So I might as well reign until September.
(September, September)
Oh, I might as well reign until September.

Inspired by: *It Might as Well Rain Until September*

Parachute Drop

5th June 2019

With the Donald we're not very fond
Of the claim that he makes "You've been conned".
But, unlike our queen,
He has never been seen
On a parachute drop with James Bond.

12. The Tory Party Leadership Context

Seven Chaps Crave Loner Idiot Test

Inspired entirely by Liam Goddard, I offer this anagram of "Conservative Leadership Contest":

Seven Chaps Crave Loner Idiot Test.

Channel 4 No-Show

18th June

Boris Johnson declined to take part in the Channel 4 leadership debate

We're not seeing that much of BoJo;
His campaign's a bit of a go-slow.
Did they keep him at home,
And remove his tweet phone,
As he watched all his Channel 4 no-show?

Shove out his Ex?

20th June

2 and 3 run the race neck and necks,
But Gove hopes to shove out his ex.
They'll ignore all the Bills
With No-Deal Happy Pills -
You'll get them from all Foreign Secs

13. European Parliament

Ode to Misery

2nd July 2019

*The Brexit MEPs turned their backs while the "Ode to Joy"
was being played.*

Yes, we realise they're singing
What they call an Ode to Joy,
But into this place we're bringing
Our intentions to destroy.
We'll be cruder,
Even ruder,
And insult the ones who work,
As we imitate our leader
Nigel Farage, foremost jerk.

We're supposed to represent you,
But instead we'll turn our backs,
Though we'll spend the salaries that
We will be paid from your tax.
Know what this bodes -
No more Joy odes -
Misery is what you'll feel.
We'll inflict this on the UK
When we bring about "No Deal".

We have got the whole thing worked out.
Trade from now will be so sweet.
As we understand the GATT rules

Which we heard that Boris tweet.
We're not bitter,
When we twitter.
What goes round will come around.
You can't hack it? Make a packet -
We'll get rich shorting the pound.

Though the British state we'll fracture,
We will drink in foreign bars.
We don't need to manufacture
Aeroplanes, machines and cars.
Oh, we're charmers,
Stuff the farmers,
We prefer pâté to lamb.
Thousands of you lose your jobs, but
Frankly we don't give a damn.

Inspired by: *Ode to Joy*

14. Boris takes charge

Oh, I'll GATT By with a Little Help from My Friends.

26th June 2019

Boris Johnson incorrectly claimed that we could continue to trade with the EU under GATT article 24 even if we had left the EU with no agreement

What would you do if I lent you some votes
To get Michael Gove out of the race?
What do you think of my speech without notes?
But you see I'm my own special case.
Oh, I'll GATT by with a little help from my friends.
Oh, I'll poll high with a little help from my friends.

What would you think if my plan made no sense?
Would you hold your nose, still vote for me?
Lend me your brain, let's not sit on the fence,
I'll say our trade will be tariff-free.
Oh, I'll GATT by with a little help from my friends.
mm, I'll poll high with a little help from my friends.
mm, gonna lie with a little help from my friends.

What do I do if you ask why I lied
To my boss or perhaps to the nation?
And then, why the questions I'm trying to hide,
From providing a full explanation?
Oh, I'll GATT by with a little help from my friends,

mm, I'll poll high with a little help from my friends,
mm, gonna lie with a little help from my friends.

Do you need tax rebate now?
I don't like facts that are real.
Let's forget the debate now.
I'd like to have a No-Deal.

What do I care for the No-Deal griefs?
For none of those griefs will be mine.
Would you believe that I'm losing my briefs?
Yes, I'm certain that it happens all the time.
Oh, I'll GATT by with a little help from my friends.
mm, I'll poll high with a little help from my friends,
mm, gonna lie with a little help from my friends

Inspired by: *I'll Get By with a Little Help From My Friends*

The Emperor with No Clothes

He talks tax cuts, but details he loathes,
And to business he offers his oaths.
Let us lay the truth bare
That the ex-London-mayor
Is an emperor who has no clothes.

Under the Bus

11ᵗʰ July 2019

*Boris Johnson was said to have thrown the UK ambassador
to the US "under the bus" by refusing to support him*

I don't know why there's so much fuss;
In "Taking control back" for us -
"How high shall we jump,
Since you ask, Mister Trump,
And who to throw under the bus?

Mars Bars and Crisps

*Boris Johnson assured us that there would still be Mars Bars
and cheese and onion crisps in the event of a "No Deal"*

Stop talking this nonsense now please -
The new Boris No-Deal wheeze
For chocolate bars
Provided from Mars
And crisps that are onion and cheese.

The levers of power he'll seize
To acquire the Number 10 keys
I hope we can stop
The unplanned cliff flop,
Or the country will be on its knees

ERG

22 July 2019

The European Research Group is publicly funded

I think it's a strange thing to see
Propaganda that's for ERG,
That's elastic on facts,
That all rigour still lacks,
And that's paid for by you and by me.

The Bus with Smiling Faces

Boris Johnson is heard on a recording negotiating with his friend as to what sort of beating they were planning for a critical journalist

Oh, I had a chat with Darius, upon the telephone,
He wanted to beat up this man who would be quite alone.
The idea was the journalist would then think to shut up
I'd got the man's address I think," I'll find it for you Gup".

Oh, my friends, the criticism's stunning;
But you can flee from justice with a little bit of cunning.
There are lots of 'lads' and 'lasses' on my bus with smiling faces,
Just like the big red bus we took to many other places.

Now Darius is my dear friend, with quite a lot of charm;
He didn't want to break a leg, or even break an arm.
No time in Intensive Care, we don't want stretcher cases.
Only two black eyes and a broken rib, and bruises in sore places.

Inspired by: *Blaydon Races*

Send in the Boris Clowns

26th July 2019

Boris Johnson assembled his Cabinet. Previous disgrace was not a disqualification.

Won't we be rich?
Is it unfair?
Priti and Gavin absolved.
They're a right pair.
There are the clowns.

Have the rest gone?
A Cabinet half.
"Unite the country" I said -
That was a laugh!
Where are the clowns?
There ought to be clowns.

Just when I'd talked,
Behind Palace doors
Finally telling the queen "This job isn't yours."
Making my entrance again with my usual flair,
Sure of my lines,
And you're all there.

Don't you love farce?
My fault, I fear;
I thought that they'd want what I want -
Sorry, Junker!
But where are the clowns?

Send in the clowns
Don't bother, they're here.

Isn't it real?
It's a No Deal.
Blaming the EU, but tardy I fear,
But where are the clowns?
There ought to be clowns
Well, maybe next year.

Inspired by: *Send in the Clowns*

Britons Never, Never, Never Shall be Fooled.

1st August 2019

When Boris fi-i-irst, and quite unplanned,
Aro-o-o-ose from out the Te-e-e-elegraph,
Arose, arose, arose from out the Te-elegraph,
He was the liar,
The liar of the land,
And wanted Bre-e-e-exit for a laugh.
Rule Britannia!
We should be well ruled.
Britons never, never, never shall be fooled.

The nations whi-i-i-ich do form EC
Won't i-i-i-i-in their turn, to Bo-o-oris fall,
Won't in their turn, to Bo-o-oris fall,
They've got the backstop,
Which Boris did agree.
No deal was never ever ever said by all.
Rule Britannia!
We should be well ruled.
Britons never, never, never shall be fooled.

Inspired by: *Rule Britannia*

15. No Deal again
Onward Brexit No-Dealers

August 2019

Onward Brexit No-Dealers,
Marching as to war.
This one's self-inflicted,
Unlike those before
But it's what we chose back then
In that famous vote.
Though it's awful, please recall
We're all in the same boat.

Dyson moved to Singapore,
How he is adored,
Rees-Mogg backing Britain but
Moved his funds abroad.
Crispin Odey placed his bets
If it goes to plan -
Tory backer makes a packet;
We go down the pan.

We will have no doom and gloom -
Optimism feel.
Don't forget, 3 years ago,
That vote for No Deal.
Or maybe it was a vote
For some small side deals,
Or Gatt-24, or maybe
What Boris reveals.

And look at the spending plans
Which have all been Boris'd.
Drawing from his dreamed-up
Fairy fiscal forest.
Food and medicine scarcer,
Quite a bitter pill,
But console yourself because
That is the People's Will.

Thankfully we chose back then
To take back control -
To our sovereign Parliament -
Oops that was own goal.
If the Parliament won't back
Plans of the top Tory,
Then perhaps let's prorogue it,
For a different story.

Well our money is worth less,
Sinking like a stone
And we'll lose our trade deals
We'll be on our own.
Turns out they weren't easy,
Turns out they are tough.
Now the borders will be harder
Crossings will be rough.

But let's have no doom and gloom.
Make the smiles large.
Even though disaster looms,
Boris is in charge.
He knows what he's doing.
Roads may have some bumps.

Ireland, trading, farming-
He will come up Trump's.

Repeat first verse

*Boris Johnson declared that Brexit would be achieved and
that there was no room for the "doomsters" and gloomsters"*
    *"The Times" headline in early August said "Boris
Johnson's donor Crispin Odey eyes Brexit jackpot with
£300m bet against British firms"*

Inspired by: *Onward Christian Soldiers*

Try A Yellow Hammer

August 2019

I've stayed at home; I've got no deal.
Now I've got to tell the EU how I feel.
If they received my letter
Telling them we'd soon be free
Then they'll know just what I'll do
If they don't want me.
I'll try a yellow hammer round the whole country.
It's been three long years; not much done you see.
If I need yellow hammers for the whole country,
It said on the bus,
Money for us.
Put blame on the EC,
If I need yellow hammers for the whole country.

So, Mr Gove, please look for me,
'Cause I couldn't bear to see what I might see.
I've still got to do Brexit and the EC holds the key.
A simple yellow hammer's what I need to set us free.
So I wrote my bolder pleas:

Whoa, try a yellow hammer round the whole country,
Will the drugs not flow, when the trade's not free?
If you have heard me saying that I now want some
respect
You'll see what I sent, the lorries in Kent, economy is
wrecked;
But I can see a yellow hammer round the whole country.

Now the whole of us are cheerin'
And I can't believe it's real -
There's sixteen yellow briefings
For our brave "No Deal".
I'm comin' home.
Try a hammer round the whole country.
Get a permit if you go EC.
Get the drugs in for an unknown fee.
Try a hammer round the whole country.

"Operation Yellowhammer" was designed to reassure the public that all would be well in the event of 'No Deal'. So far it has probably done exactly the opposite.

Inspired by: *Tie a Yellow Ribbon*

Denmark

August 2019

President Trump took offence when Denmark refused to sell Greenland, and cancelled a state visit to Denmark

With Denmark, Trump now wants to dis it.
So, here's what I want to know: "Is it
Required that it's planned
To sell Trump some land
If you're hoping he'll pay you a visit?"

Remainers Unite!

August 2019

If the driver's deranged at the wheel,
Then it's up to the others I feel
To get the wrongs righted
By being united
In leading away from "No Deal".

Thirty Days
August 2019

Boris Johnson had talks with Angela Merkel and emerged looking optimistically at solving the Irish border question within 30 days.

On the time that it takes to find ways
For resolving the Irish maze
And clearing the row -
They'd have done it by now
If all that they need's thirty days.

'Till Borisma Drives The Backstop Far Away

23 August 2019

We'll meet again,
Don't know why,
Don't know when.
But I know we'll meet again some summit day.
I'm bluffing through
Until we leave EU,
Till Borisma* drives the backstop far away.

So, will you please say hello
To Varadkar and co,
Tell them I'm never wrong,
30 days, don't you know,
What a blistering show,
Good grief that is not long.

We'll meet again,
Don't know why,
Don't know when.
But I know we'll meet again some summit day,
We'll meet again,
Don't know why,
Don't know when.
But I know we'll meet again some summit day.
I'm bluffing through,
Until we leave EU,
Till Borisma drives the backstop far away

So, don't read all the news -
It's not true that I'll lose,
Though my lead is not large,
I'm ignoring their pleas,
I'm suspending MPs,
And I only fear Farage.

We'll meet again,
Don't know why,
Don't know when.
But I know we'll meet again some summit day.

* *Borisma – Boris Johnson charisma. By his own estimation this is very powerful.*

Inspired by: *We'll Meet Again*

Though I've Listened Long Enough to You

August 2019

Message to Boris Johnson

Though I've listened long enough to you,
There's no way to believe that it's all true,
Knowing that you lied, straight-faced, while we cried;
So, I look to find a person to believe.

Someone like you makes me want to look
For somebody else.
Someone like you makes it easy to see
You're thinking about yourself.

If you knew the country's changed its mind,
Must find a way just to leave the past behind,
Knowing that you lied, straight-faced, while we cried.
So, I look to find a person to believe.

Though I've listened long enough to you
There's no way to believe that it's all true,
Knowing that you lied, straight-faced, while we cried;
So, I look to find a person to believe.

Inspired by: *Reason to Believe*

16. Cummings, Rees-Mogg and Proroguing

The Consensus of Cummings

29 August 2019

Boris Johnson initiated a request to prorogue Parliament for five weeks, but he and his Minister declined to be questioned on this. This was after he sought to summon up the votes of the Tory Party membership with the following paragraph:

"I would also like to make it absolutely clear that I am not attracted to arcane procedures such as the prorogation of Parliament. As someone who aspires to be Prime Minister of a democratic nation, I believe in finding consensus in the House of Commons."

Please bear with my media shunnings
While I cancel most Parliament runnings.
In my letter of summons
"Consensus of Commons"
Should have read "the Consensus of Cummings".

We're Off to See the Cummings

30 August 2019
Dominic Cummings sacked a Treasury Special Adviser, confiscated her pass and she was escorted out of 10 Downing Street by armed police.

We're off to see the Cummings,
The powerful Cummings of Boz.
We hear he is a whiz of a Dom,
If ever a Dom there was.
If ever, oh ever a Dom there was,
The Cummings of Boz is one because,
Because, because, because, because, because,
Because of ingenious things he does.

We've been to see the Cummings,
The masterful Cummings of Boz.
D'you hear he has a whizz of a plan?
It's very clever because -
Well never, oh never, d'you shut the House
For five long weeks until they rouse.
But Dom told Boz, do this, because,
There was a plot, indeed there was.

We went to see the Cummings
The Cummings and Goings of Boz.
We know he sacks whoever he likes,
And off they go with the rozz.
Your pass into the bin he'll toss.
And if you ask "I'm sacked because?"
"Because, because, because, because, because"
Because Cummings does things the way he does.

Inspired by: *We're Off to See the Wizard*

As Long Jacob Slumbered

4 Sept 2019

I wondered, as long Jacob slumbered,
How long, with these toffs, we are lumbered.
But look what they've done -
They have sacked twenty-one.
So their days are undoubtedly numbered.

Twenty-One

4 Sept 2019

Twenty-one could not have been wronger
So I can't stand them here any longer.
Enough of their lip;
We'll remove the Whip
Ah - now I am feeling much stronge

Early Election

4 Sept 2019

With confident superiority,
But lacking sufficient authority,
On polling projection,
Call early election,
Like Theresa, to get your majority.

Rees-Mogg Takes You Down

6 Sept 2019

Rees-Mogg takes you down,
To his place near the tower,
Where he lounges on the benches,
And with Parliamentary power,
He sends insults to the doctor
Who worked on Yellowhammer,
And compares to Andrew Wakefield
Who caused autism clamour,
Who caused kids to die from measles.
Well the doctor shouted, "Do you
Want to say the words in public?
Because if you do I'll sue you."
Rees-Mogg's always been aloofer.
You don't want to Leave here with him.
You don't want to travel blind,
And you know that you can't trust him.
He's not pushed his dreadful claptrap to your mind.

And Boris is a liar,
And they tried to keep him quiet
In the leadership election,
And they hoped people would buy it,
And they made him Tory leader,
Thought they had nobody better,
And he talked about the deadline
In EU extension letter,
And he said that in October,
Done or not, we would be going,

And in "negotiations"
There was no progress showing,
As he's not an EU lover.
You don't want to Leave here with him.
You don't want to travel blind,
And you know that you can't trust him.
He's not pushed his dreadful claptrap to your mind.

And Boris said he wouldn't
Stop the Parliament from sitting,
But he'd already decided,
Tell the Queen that it is fitting
To send MPs away because
There's nothing needing rigour
From MPs applying challenge
With their customary vigour.
But within the Tory party,
Twenty-one of them are saner,
Though expelled because they don't see
That No-Deal's a No-Brainer.
So Boris sacked those wiser.
You don't want to Leave here with him.
You don't want to travel blind,
And you know that you can't trust him.
He's not pushed his dreadful claptrap to your mind.

After the doctor in question threatened to sue if Jacob Rees-Mogg repeated the slur outside Parliament, Jacob-Rees-Mogg apologised for insulting the doctor. The original insult was made in the House of Commons under Parliamentary privilege.

Inspired by: *Suzanne*

I am the Very Model of a Prejudiced Etonian

By Robin Wallington
7 Sept 2019

I am the very model of a prejudiced Etonian.
My diction is impeccable, my politics draconian,
I'm quite the polar opposite of what you'd call revisionist,
And though I went to public school, at least I'm not a Wykehamist.
I'm keeping the tradition of the gentry ent'ring politics,
How else are we to keep away the Corbynista Bolsheviks?
So through my vivid promises of dividends most decorous,
I've mobilised the Brexiteers to levels quite obstreperous,
I whip them up to frenzy in a manner so Pavlovian.
They do not seem to see that it's increasingly dystopian,
So here I stand before you like a skeletal Napoleon,
I am the very model of a prejudiced Etonian.

I've studied all the Classics from Herodotus to Sophocles.
How else am I to criticise my colleagues' etymologies?
Perhaps that's why I vote against most freedoms and equalities.
These authors are about as old as most of my philosophies!
I know of all the backwards Parliament'ry curiosities.
Like letting Commons' priv'lege keep me safe to spout atrocities.
I know the terminologies, chronologies and glossaries.
And yet I still behave as if we never lost the colonies.
I often drain the public funds to renovate my properties,
Although I have more money than some smaller world economies.
I never make apologies for lack of reciprocities,
Despite the fact that swathes of Britons lack basic commodities!

My views on social issues haven't changed much since the Tudor times.
I rage against the slightest change to long-outdated paradigms.
I lack the base ability to sympathise or empathise.
My Commons' sprawl exemplifies the privilege I symbolise.
When criticised on Women's Rights I hide behind Catholicism,
Bending it to justify my heart-of-stone Conservatism,
Yet I sound the clarion of fear of fundamentalism.
Without seeming to acknowledge this inherent dualism,
I try to paint a picture of a Brexit most utopian,
And when they all explain to me the likely pandemonium,
I patronise my critics with my methods Ciceronian,
I am the very model of a prejudiced Etonian.

Inspired by: *I am the very model of a modern Major-General*

Government's Leader Says Government's Busy

10 September 2019

The Government prorogued Parliament last night.

Government's leader says Government's busy,
Too busy to meet for five weeks.
Government's leader says Government's trying,
To start with a brand-new Queen's speech.
Government's leader says Government's happy,
Now that they're well out of reach.
And the Commons Speaker says thirty days out
Is outrageous ...action ...
Please Mr Johnson, we just want some scrutiny,
Only wanted a while.
Please Mr Johnson, we just want to tell you goodbye.

Government's leader says Government's hiding
Reports that the others still seek.
Government's leader says Government's saying,
We'll not say too much on the leak.
Government's leader says Government's ready,
To break the law we passed this week.
And the Commons Speaker says thirty days out
Is outrageous ...action..
Please Mr Johnson, we just want some scrutiny,
Only wanted a while.
Please Mr Johnson, we just want to tell you goodbye.

Government's leader says Government wants to
Escape from their Parliament's gaze.
Government's leader says Government's hurrying,
For a Deal as they had 30 days.
Government's leader says grant an election,
And later we'll outline the ways.
And the Commons Speaker says thirty days out
Is outrageous ...action ...
Please Mr Johnson, we just want some scrutiny,
Only wanted a while.
Please Mr Johnson, we just want to tell you goodbye.

Inspired by: *Sylvia's Mother*

17. Last Word (for now)

I Dreamed a Dream

15 Sept 2019

DAVID CAMERON ON BREXIT summarised

There was a time Michael was kind,
Boris' thinking was strong.
And they weren't complaining.
There was a time we weren't behind,
And they'd play along,
And they backed Remaining
There was a time -
Then it all went wrong.

I dreamed a dream in times gone by,
When hope was high for referendum.
I dreamed, that Tory doubts would die,
As with the vote, at last we'd end 'em.
Then I was young, it's true to tell.
Speeches were made, who'll be my backer?
Fed up with Priti Patel,
But still I feared I couldn't sack her.

With the Cummings of the night,
Michael Gove said no more experts.
With their warnings by the Right,
Were they winning with their race?
We slept that summer, were not wise;
"Be filled with a million guest Turks?"

They sent the adverts with the lies,
Which then were gone from Book of Face.

And still I dream of the EC -
A second vote, perhaps, I feel.
But there are dreams that cannot be,
As Boris drives towards No Deal.
I had a dream the vote would be,
So different from that hell of lying,
So different from these Brexit memes;
And now they've killed the dream
I dreamed.

Inspired by: *"I dreamed a dream"*, *Les Misérables*.

Reference
Index of titles

As Long Jacob Slumbered, 116
Brexit Alphabet, 10
Brexit Cokey, 13
Brexit Game, 49
Brexit Mia, 47
Brexit Pie, 33
Brexit's a Trick, not a Treat?, 72
Brexitian Fantasy, 5
Brexit's Coming Home, 53
Britons Never, Never, Never Shall be Fooled, 104
Bus With Smiling Faces, 101
Channel 4 No-Show, 94
Consensus of Cummings, 114
Could We Start Again Please?, 44
Cricket Scoreboard, 12
Dance for the Deal, 80
Denmark, 110
Doh, We're Here, 72
Don't Cry For Leave Now, Theresa, 45
Early Election, 116
Emperor With No Clothes, 99
ERG, 100
EU Responds to Article 50., 26
Final Say, 91
First No Deal, 78
Government's Leader Says Government's Busy, 121
How Do You Solve A Problem Like Our Brexit?, 66

I Beg My Pardon, 31
I Dreamed a Dream, 123
I Might as Well Reign until September., 92
I'm Just A Girl Who Cain't Say "Go", 64
It's My Brexit and I'll Cry if I Want to, 63
Knowing Me Knowing EU, 24
Maggie May, 28
Many Votes of Brexit, 87
Mars Bars and Crisps, 100
Menu for EU Summit Dinner, 89
Nineteenth Brexit Breakdown, 59
Now She Is A Leaver, 22
Ode To Misery, 95
Oh I'll GATT By with a Little Help from My Friends., 97
Oh Theresa First Looked Out, 74
Once More onto the Pitch, Dear Friends, Once More, 57
Onward Brexit No-Dealers, 105
Our Way, 8
Parachute Drop, 93
Port-A-Loo, 70
Rees-Mogg Takes You Down, 117
Remain Lied Too, 16
Remainers Unite!, 110
Rock Paper Scissors, 73
Round - Like a Brexit Without Exit, 51
Say Goodbye Our Former Partner, 41
Send in the Boris Clowns, 102
Seven Chaps Crave Loner Idiot Test, 94
Shove out his Ex?, 94
Sit on the Fence, 91
Take a Chance on Me, 84

They Said There'll Be Deals at Brexit, 82
Thirty Days, 110
This Time, 53
Though I've Listened Long Enough To You, 113
'Till Borisma Drives The Backstop Far Away, 111
Trumpet So Wide, 61
Try A Yellow Hammer, 108
Twenty-One, 116
Under the Bus, 99
We're Off to See the Cummings, 115
Whatever Happened To The Brexit Deal?, 68
When The Nightmare Is Over, 38
Where Have All Of UKIP Gone?, 43
You're Got Brexit, Needing an Exit, 83
You're in EU, Going for Exit, 20

Index of references to original songs

American Pie, 33

Blaydon Races, 101

Bohemian Rhapsody, 5

Could We start Again, Please, 44

Dance for Your Daddy, 80

Doe, a Deer, 72

Don't Cry for Me, Argentina, 45

First Noel, 78

Football's Coming Home, 55

Hokey-Cokey, 13

How do you solve a problem like Maria?, 66

I am the very model of a modern Major-General, 119

I Dreamed a Dream, 123

I Will Survive, 26

I'll Get By with a Little Help From My Friends, 97

I'm a Believer, 22

I'm Just a Girl who Caint Say "No", 64

It Might As Well Rain Until September, 92

It's My Party and I'll Cry if I Want To, 63

Knowing Me, Knowing You, 24

Lord Chancellor's Song, 38

Maggie May, 28

Mama Mia, 47

My Way, 8

Nineteenth Nervous Breakdown, 59

Ode to Joy, 95

Oh, What Happened to You?, 68

Once more unto the breach, 57

Onward Christian Soldiers, 105

Reason to Believe, 113
Rose Garden, 31
Rule Britannia, 104
Send In the Clowns, 102
She Loves You, 16
Suzanne, 117
Sylvia's Mother, 121
Take a Chance on Me, 84
They Said There'll Be Snow at Christmas, 82
This Time, 53
Ticket To Ride, 61
Tie a Yellow Ribbon, 108
Twelve Days of Christmas, 87
Waterloo, 70
We'll Meet Again, 111
We're Off to See the Wizard, 115
Whatever Happened to the Likely Lads, 68
When the Boat Comes In, 80
When the Carnival is Over, 41
Where Have All the Flowers Gone?, 43
Windmills of Your Mind, 51
You are Sixteen, Going on Seventeen, 20, 83

What Others Have Said About the Songs in this Book

"Needs to go viral!"

"That's brilliant! So funny I just sang it all out loud!"

"You're a flipping genius!"

"This Is Very Good!!"

"Made my day! Thanks."

"Brilliant - I'm sharing."

"Absolutely marvellous! Gilbert would be proud!"

"I was literally reading it while singing!"

"Very clever. I don't think the original will ever sound the same!"

"Absolutely brilliant!" ☺☺

Printed in Great Britain
by Amazon